D1732746

REAL TEENS... REAL ISSUES

DEPRESSION AND STRESS

Katie Marsico

Cavendish
Square
New York

The author would like to dedicate this book to Nicole, Paige, and Anthony, and the other members of the K.A.T. Foundation. She extends her sincere gratitude to her editor, Christine Florie, whose support and guidance in writing this book proved invaluable.

To protect the privacy of sources, only first names are used throughout the book. Any first names that are asterisked (*) indicate the use of a pseudonym.

Published in 2014 by Cavendish Square Publishing, LLC
303 Park Avenue South, Suite 1247, New York, NY 10010

Copyright © 2014 by Cavendish Square Publishing, LLC

First Edition

Website: cavendishsq.com

This publication represents the opinions and views of the author based on his or her personal experience, knowledge, and research. The information in this book serves as a general guide only. The author and publisher have used their best efforts in preparing this book and disclaim liability rising directly or indirectly from the use and application of this book.

CPSIA Compliance Information: Batch #WS13CSQ

All websites were available and accurate when this book was sent to press.

LIBRARY OF CONGRESS CATALOGING-IN-PUBLICATION DATA
Marsico, Katie, 1980–
Depression and stress / Katie Marsico.
p. cm. — (Real teens ... real issues)
Includes bibliographical references and index.
Summary: "Provides comprehensive information on depression and stress, including first-person interviews, signs and symptoms, physical dangers, recovery, and solutions"—Provided by publisher.
ISBN 978-1-60870-851-2 (hardcover) ISBN 978-1-62712-127-9 (paperback)
ISBN 978-1-60870-857-4 (ebook)
1. Depression in adolescence—Juvenile literature. 2. Stress in adolescence. I. Title.
RJ506.D4M287 2013
618.92'8527—dc23
2011016705

EDITOR: Christine Florie
ART DIRECTOR: Anahid Hamparian   SERIES DESIGNER: Kristen Branch

EXPERT READER: Benjamin L. Hankin, Ph.D., associate professor, Department of Psychology, University of Denver

Photo research by Marybeth Kavanagh
Title page illustration by Corinne Florie

Printed in the United States of America

CONTENTS

It is not uncommon for people struggling with stress or depression to mask their emotions.

ONE

HiDING UNDER THE "HAPPY MASK"

LOOKING BACK, EIGHTEEN-YEAR-OLD Nicole says that she "was always a worrier." Yet she also admits that she was good at putting on what she describes as a "happy mask." By high school, she had established a reputation in her Illinois community as a successful student and varsity track star. As a result of what they saw on the surface, few of Nicole's peers or family members had any real idea of all that her happy mask hid.

Underneath the straight As and the impressive athletic performances was a severely depressed and stressed teenager. During middle school, Nicole had developed an eating disorder. Toward the end of her sophomore year of high school, she had started to cut herself with razor blades. For Nicole, slicing her skin open was a means of punishing herself.

"I like people thinking I'm perfect," she admits. "But even being a straight-A student was not good enough if I didn't get 100 percent on everything. So I punished myself by not eating and, later, by cutting. Through it all, I was always smiling, but, deep down, that's not how it was."

> "Through it all, I was always smiling, but, deep down, that's not how it was."
> — Nicole

In fact, Nicole felt the exact opposite of a happy, confident young adult. While her class-mates were discussing colleges and relationships, she was making other plans. They weren't definite at first, but by late May 2010, she had a clear idea of how she would shape her future.

"I rode my bike to a local bridge that stretched over traffic that was traveling about 60 miles per hour. I mounted the railing and sat there for three hours as I prepared to dive into the cars and trucks beneath me." What ultimately stopped Nicole from taking the plunge that would have prevented her from living to tell her story?

It is easy for people to become wrapped up in the stress and pressure that surrounds them.

> "When you're depressed, you have such a narrow picture of what's going on and what your priorities should be."
> — Nicole

"It suddenly occurred to me that I still had a math final to complete," she explains. "I had just spent twenty hours studying for that test and didn't want to miss it. When you're depressed, you have such a narrow picture of what's going on and what your priorities should be. My desire to do well on that math test is what saved my life."

In the days that followed, Nicole's mother realized what was going on and took her to the local emergency room. Nicole now perceives this moment as the turning point in her battle with depression and stress. While in the emergency room, Nicole opened up about her struggle with depression and the anxiety of trying to live up to her own impossible standards of perfection. Over the next few months, she participated in a program to help her deal with these issues. She continues to see a counselor and a psychiatrist to make sure that depression and stress never control so much of her life again.

"When I was at my worst with these problems, it was kind of like another person took over my identity," Nicole reflects. "Now I'm seventeen and have only recently started to understand that my depression and the mask I wore to hide it never really allowed me to have a childhood."

"Now I'm seventeen and have only recently started to understand that my depression and the mask I wore to hide it never really allowed me to have a childhood."
— **Nicole**

AN OVERVIEW OF DEPRESSION AND STRESS

Nicole's story may sound shocking, but it is not unique. Teens often hear that their entire futures lie ahead of them, but some find it unbearable to look beyond the intense pressure and pain that shape their day-to-day lives. Depression and stress are emotional reactions that people of all ages frequently experience when they are unable to cope with triggers ranging from sudden trauma to long-term tension.

According to youth-development experts at the University of Minnesota in Minneapolis, stress is a

STARTLING STAT

A RECENT STUDY REVEALED THAT 68 PERCENT OF TEEN-AGERS FELT SCHOOLWORK WAS THE LEADING CAUSE OF THEIR STRESS.

condition that "is characterized by feelings of tension, frustration, worry, sadness, and withdrawal that commonly last from a few hours to a few days." Depression "is characterized by more extreme feelings of hopelessness, sadness, isolation, worry, withdrawal, and worthlessness that last for two weeks or more." For someone who has a major depressive disorder—which is also referred to as **clinical depression**—these symptoms tend to be especially severe. The emotional distress that accompanies clinical depression typically disrupts a person's ability to function in and enjoy day-to-day life.

Severe stress can result in similar problems. Like depression, it is at the root of several mental-health conditions, including anxiety disorders. In addition, stress can trigger depression and vice versa. It is important to remember that not everyone dealing

Many people experience sadness and stress when confronted with certain triggers.

with these issues has identical symptoms—or any obvious symptoms at all. Like Nicole, many people who are affected by serious depression or stress become skilled at masking their emotions.

11

THE SCOPE OF A TROUBLING TEEN ISSUE

Research shows that approximately 20 percent of U.S. teens are struggling with clinical depression. Experts believe that almost 10 percent of teens have an anxiety disorder.

What exactly do these statistics mean for teenagers living with severe depression or stress? For people who don't receive or respond to treatment, the end result can be fatal. Suicide is the third-leading cause of death for people between the ages of fifteen and twenty-four.

According to Claudia Welke, MD, these sometimes shocking statistics are probably affected by a combination of factors. Welke is a psychiatrist and the director of child and adolescent training at North

STARTLING STAT

RESEARCH INDICATES THAT AS MANY AS 8.3 PERCENT OF TEENS STRUGGLE WITH DEPRESSION FOR AT LEAST TWELVE MONTHS AT A TIME.

According to the Experts

As a psychiatrist, Doctor Welke grasps that serious depression and anxiety are not as black and white as they may initially seem. For example, she explains that some of the feelings that go hand in hand with emotional problems and disorders are not always necessarily "bad."

"We all actually need some stress and anxiety," she says. "It motivates us to set goals, finish projects, and show up places on time. [However,] when kids find themselves so overwhelmed that they can't . . . go to school or start their homework, it's a real problem."

Shore University Health System, in Highland Park, Illinois. She is also a clinical instructor at the University of Chicago Pritzker School of Medicine, in Chicago, Illinois.

"Are we seeing more depression and anxiety among teenagers because we now know how to better identify these problems?" Welke ponders. "Or are they more common mental-health conditions because the world today is more stressful in general? I'd say that the answer to both questions is yes."

TUMBLING INTO TURMOIL

Seventeen-year-old Anthony can pinpoint the start of his battle with clinical depression to a loss that shook his world in 2009. That year, his best friend committed suicide—an event that left the Tennessee teen struggling with overwhelming feelings of exhaustion and loneliness. Anthony describes the period that followed as one in which he was "really down all the time."

"I didn't know what to do with myself," he explains. "I was always sad, and I was . . . just lost." As his depression and stress deepened, Anthony grew disinterested in his schoolwork. His personal relationships also began to suffer. While Anthony

STARTLING STAT

MENTAL-HEALTH EXPERTS BELIEVE THAT TEENS SUFFER-
ING FROM UNTREATED DEPRESSION ARE UP TO TWELVE
TIMES MORE LIKELY TO COMMIT SUICIDE THAN THOSE
WHO ARE NOT.

would still go out with his friends, he admits that he rarely enjoyed himself and was usually quiet and withdrawn.

"To be honest, day-to-day life was . . . exhausting," he says. "I mean, being down all the time while everyone else around me seemed happy and joyful just got old—and it got old fast." Anthony decided to start therapy for his depression a few months after it began.

> "I didn't know what to do with myself. I was always sad, and I was . . . just lost."
> —Anthony

He has a few ideas, based on his personal experiences, about what causes people to fall into a cycle of sadness and stress. On the one hand, he recognizes that his friend's suicide triggered his depression.

16

One sign of depression is withdrawal from social and personal relationships.

Yet Anthony also feels that several other factors put people his age at risk for becoming seriously depressed or anxious. He suspects that a lot of teenagers don't open up about their feelings because they don't want to be labeled as "having a problem."

"I think depression and stress are huge problems that affect the average American teenager," he reflects. "When teens these days get upset . . . they [often] keep it in and don't talk about what's bothering them. Then one thing leads to another and . . . before they know it, they have huge problems on their hands."

RECOGNIZING RISK FACTORS

The roots of the "huge problems" that lead to severe depression and stress often vary from person to person. In most situations, it's likely that a combination of

STARTLING STAT

RESEARCH INDICATES THAT BETWEEN 20 AND 50 PERCENT OF TEENS DEALING WITH CLINICAL DEPRESSION HAVE A FAMILY HISTORY OF EITHER THAT CONDITION OR OTHER MENTAL-HEALTH PROBLEMS.

individual circumstances and the larger social influences that Anthony mentions place people at risk for
developing these conditions. For some sufferers, an
imbalance of brain chemicals can trigger disorders related to depression or stress. Doctors also believe that
someone with a family history of such conditions is
at a greater risk for developing a disorder, as well.

In other cases, a particularly traumatic event,
such as parents divorcing or a friend dying, can cause

Living in an unhappy home can cause stress
and depression.

significant stress and depression. The same can be said of physical, emotional, or sexual abuse. In addition, a variety of comorbid conditions—including learning disabilities, eating disorders, and drug and alcohol addiction—leave people more vulnerable to depression and anxiety.

"There is not one single factor that accounts for teen depression [and anxiety]," explains George Sachs. Doctor Sachs, a licensed clinical psychologist, is the founder of the Sachs Center in New York City. This treatment facility addresses a variety of behavioral, developmental, and emotional conditions, including depression and anxiety. "Just because you have experienced one of the factors, or stressors, that trigger depression and anxiety does not necessarily mean you will develop these conditions. However, the more stressors you experience, the more support you will need to effectively cope."

In addition to the individual circumstances that make a person more likely to become seriously

"[T]he more stressors you experience, the more support you will need to effectively cope."

—George Sachs, PsyD

Academic pressure is one cause of stress and depression.

depressed or stressed, adolescence itself can also serve as a risk factor. Most people experience major physical and emotional stresses during this time in their lives. Changes in hormones, as well as the forming of new relationships and pressure to excel in school shape the way teenagers view and respond to the world around them.

It is therefore not uncommon for teens to feel confused, lonely, worried, and frustrated. Yet, while it is perfectly normal for everyone to experience these emotions at one time or another, not dealing with them can result in more severe depression or stress. Many people fear the social **stigma** of discussing or seeking help for any mental-health issues. Some also believe, incorrectly, that not being able to solve a problem or simply cheer up on one's own is a sign of weakness and immaturity.

CLUES THAT SUGGEST A SERIOUS CONDITION

Though Anthony remembers his family and friends becoming concerned about him in 2009, the warning signs of clinical depression and anxiety can be difficult to spot, the reason being that they frequently vary from person to person. It can also be challenging to distinguish between serious depression and stress and a passing case of the blues and normal tension. Most experts suggest seeking help if someone exhibits certain behaviors or attitudes for longer than two weeks.

Signs frequently include intense displays of anger, sadness, or hopelessness. Teens who are experiencing serious depression or stress may overreact to criticism, cry more than usual, or become agitated for

A few signs of depression and stress are sadness, hopelessness, and a lack of concentration.

Avoid Assumptions!

Just because someone doesn't specifically talk about suicide doesn't mean that individual is not suicidal. As Anthony explains, it's important to pay close attention to words or actions that might hint at a person's sinking deeper into dangerous depression or anxiety.

"I don't know if I was ever 'suicidal,'" he says. "But one weekend I got so upset that I told my other friends, 'I don't want to be here anymore—I want to leave and leave all the pain behind.' That's what triggered them to tell my parents. That's what got me the help I needed, and that's why I fought depression and won."

no reason. They might complain of being tired all the time or unable to concentrate.

Further warning signs of a need to receive treatment for depression or stress may be apparent in a student's academic performance and social life. A student might suddenly appear unmotivated or disinterested in his or her grades. People who are severely depressed or anxious will also often withdraw from social activities that once gave them pleasure. It is not uncommon for such individuals to have sudden changes in their appetite and sleep patterns, as well.

In addition, many people who are clinically depressed or anxious demonstrate low self-esteem, often describing themselves as worthless or incapable of reaching certain expectations. Some even discuss or joke about the possibility of suicide. Such hints should never be treated lightly or ignored, especially if they are accompanied by other symptoms of depression or anxiety.

THREE

FEELING THE MENTAL AND PHYSICAL EFFECTS

DURING HER SOPHOMORE YEAR OF high school, seventeen-year-old Paige began experiencing what she describes as "periods of emotional instability." According to the Illinois teen, she felt as if she was always "running on an empty battery." She started showing up late to certain classes and even failed math, despite the fact that she was constantly studying.

Paige insists that no single traumatic event triggered her stress and depression, though she acknowledges that she's always been a perfectionist. After her freshman year of high school, this personality trait was put to the test by what she perceived as tougher

STARTLING STAT

RESEARCHERS SAY THAT ABOUT 19 PERCENT OF TEENAGE GIRLS WHO REPORT BEING STRESSED REFUSE TO ADDRESS THE SOURCE OF THEIR ANXIETY.

academic expectations. As a sophomore, Paige struggled to manage her time and balance her class load with after-school sports such as volleyball and softball. The realization that her parents were having marital problems further fueled her unhappiness.

By Paige's junior year of high school, the periods of intense stress and depression were impacting not just her mind but her body as well. Despite her best attempts to keep her anxiety in check, she suddenly began having panic attacks in which she would "**hyperventilate** in complete anxiety, embarrassment, and insecurity." In her junior year, Paige began suffering from panic attacks that she says left her feeling "defeated, depleted, and depressed all at once."

"During . . . my panic attacks, my mind goes blank," she notes. "I can only think, feel, and breathe the phrase, 'I can't.' When my negative thoughts get out of control, my body takes the toll, and I normally

Sometimes severe stress can lead to crippling panic attacks.

"When my negative thoughts get out of control, my body takes the toll. . . . I'm just physically taking the pain that my mind has caused."

— Paige

succumb to this 'here we go again' notion. I'm not scared in that moment—I'm just physically taking the pain that my mind has caused."

THE LINK BETWEEN BODY AND MIND

Panic attacks are one of several physical side effects

that can result from severe anxiety. How the body responds to the mental distress caused by severe anxiety or clinical depression varies from person to person. Yet people who are seriously depressed or stressed tend to share certain physical symptoms.

"It is not unusual for patients suffering from anxiety issues to have a racing heartbeat," says Doctor Welke. "Other physical symptoms might include sweaty palms and gastrointestinal [stomach] problems." High blood pressure and rapid breathing that sometimes develops into hyperventilation are also common side effects of severe stress. Welke notes that patients struggling with clinical depression frequently have lower than normal energy levels and a decreased appetite.

Other physical responses to these conditions include acne, hair loss, unexplained muscle pain, and headaches. Many patients mention experiencing sleep disruptions and being less able to fight off sickness. Many find that medical problems that existed before they became depressed or anxious worsen. For instance, people with asthma sometimes report that they have more difficulty breathing during periods of stress or depression.

One physical response to stress and depression is the inability to sleep.

Why do mental conditions trigger such a wide variety of physical symptoms? For starters, doctors believe that being depressed or stressed slows down certain bodily processes. A slowing down of the digestion process, for example, can cause stomach and appetite problems. Doctors also suspect that the imbalanced brain chemicals that sometimes trigger severe depression and stress might affect the way people experience pain and discomfort.

STARTLING STAT

A RECENT STUDY SHOWS THAT 77 PERCENT OF
AMERICANS COMPLAIN ABOUT EXPERIENCING PHYSICAL
SYMPTOMS AS A RESULT OF THEIR STRESS.

IMPACTS ON MOOD
AND MENTAL HEALTH

Clinical depression and stress do far more than make a person feel a little sad or anxious. These mental conditions interfere with the ability of sufferers to enjoy a normal, productive life. For people who are expected to focus during class, be confident and social outside of school, and successfully plan their futures, depression and anxiety can be devastating.

As their emotional distress deepens, many develop problems with self-cutting, substance abuse, or eating disorders. Others attempt—and sometimes successfully commit—suicide. It is important to understand that people suffering from depression and anxiety often feel disconnected from those around them. Compared with parents and peers, they

31

A Significant Student Issue

"High school has always been extremely difficult for me," Paige says. "Beginning freshman year, I had very unrealistic academic expectations. I was always striving for straight As, but there were some classes where I just couldn't get them. As a result, I started feeling defeated very early on."

After a while, Paige's unhappiness spilled over into her athletic performance, as well. "It's easy to forget why you become involved in these sports in the first place," she says. "All of my panic attacks have occurred during sports. I think this is probably because my negative thoughts circulate fastest in fast-paced atmospheres."

may be experiencing overwhelming emotional pain or a frightening sense of numbness.

On the one hand, the slightest bump in the road can prompt a person living with serious depression or anxiety to overreact with extreme anger, sadness, or frustration. In other cases, someone who is dealing with these conditions may hardly show any response to situations that normally trigger emotions such as sorrow or happiness. Self-injury, eating disorders,

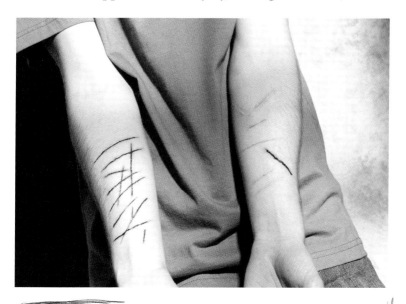

Some teens develop severe depression and stress that results in self-cutting.

and drug and alcohol abuse can therefore become unhealthy methods of either blocking out or creating certain feelings. Even if such problems don't surface, depression and anxiety inevitably take an enormous toll on the relationships and social lives of those who suffer with these disorders.

FOUR

ROUGH ON RELATIONSHIPS

EIGHTEEN-YEAR-OLD NICOLE ADMITS that there are still moments when depression and anxiety cloud her relationships with the people around her. She says she feels more comfortable talking about her emotions now than she did when her problems started. Yet the Illinois teen continues to struggle with the idea that her friends and family can and should care about her.

"It's hard to keep asking for support from everyone," Nicole explains. "I don't really feel like I deserve friendship,

> "It's hard to keep asking for support from everyone. I don't really feel like I deserve friendship, love, and kindness."
> — Nicole

35

Some people have difficulty communicating their feelings of sadness and stress, resulting in the breakdown of relationships with those who care about them most.

love, and kindness." She acknowledges that building honest, open relationships with her parents and friends was not the most important thing on her mind when her depression and anxiety were at their worst. Instead, Nicole dedicated most of her energy to putting on a happy face while she battled deep

STARTLING STAT

RECENT RESEARCH INDICATES THAT 41 PERCENT OF
WOMEN LIVING WITH DEPRESSION ARE TOO EMBARRASSED
TO SEEK HELP.

sadness and stress that ultimately fueled an eating disorder and self-cutting.

"I admitted some of my problems to my mom, but I lied about how long they had been going on," Nicole says. "When my mother made me see a school counselor, I didn't take it very seriously. I basically [lied] my way though most of the sessions." Meanwhile, depression and anxiety took a stronger and stronger grip on her mood and ability to function in day-to-day situations.

"[Those issues] started to control everything," she reflects. "Depression and stress seemed to influence

> "Depression and stress seemed to influence every area of my life, from how I read books and wrote papers to how little I enjoyed myself at parties."
> — **Nicole**

every area of my life, from how I read books and wrote papers to how little I enjoyed myself at parties."

MENTAL ISSUES THAT ISOLATE

One of the most tragic effects of clinical depression and anxiety is the toll that these conditions take on the sufferers' ability to build and maintain healthy relationships. For someone struggling with depression or anxiety, intense and confusing emotions often lead to feelings of isolation and anger. It is not unusual for sufferers to think that no one truly understands what they are going through. As a result, they frequently withdraw from social situations that once gave them pleasure. Family gatherings, school events, dates, and time with friends become more of a chore than a chance to hang out and have fun.

Such individuals may also be more vulnerable to new relationships and influences that have a harmful impact on their lives. For example, people who are severely depressed or anxious might turn to drugs or alcohol as a way of coping with their emotional pain and confusion. Some develop eating disorders or problems with cutting. Others may become involved in relationships that result in physical, emotional, or sexual abuse.

Sometimes people turn to drugs or alcohol as a way to deal with their pain.

STARTLING STAT

During one mental-health study conducted recently, 45 percent of teens between the ages of thirteen and seventeen said they felt more stressed than the year before. Yet only 28 percent of parents observed this change in their children.

People who know someone battling clinical depression or stress may notice some of these shifts in attitude and behavior, but they might not be aware of what is causing them. As a result, family and friends are frequently hurt by behaviors they don't fully understand. Unsurprisingly, the secrecy and lies that many people depend on to hide their emotional troubles only further complicate their personal relationships.

WHY IT'S HARD TO ASK FOR HELP

There are numerous reasons why sufferers choose to conceal severe depression and stress rather than reach out and seek help from friends and family members. They are often afraid of how their image and identity

"Sometimes teens isolate themselves because they do not want to be seen as different or as failures for not managing [their lives] better."
— George Sachs, PsyD

will change if they are labeled as having a mental-health issue. Many worry that people around them will view their condition as evidence that they are unable to solve their own problems. As Doctor Sachs explains, shutting out friends and family this way usually causes depression and stress to worsen.

"Sometimes teens isolate themselves because they do not want to be seen as different or as failures for not managing [their lives] better," he says. "This can result in their feeling even more unsupported and alone."

What such sufferers do not realize is that it is unsafe to assume that serious depression and stress will disappear without some form of treatment. If and when family and friends finally realize that someone in their life needs help, things may already have reached a dangerous boiling point. Self-destructive

Another Person's Point of View

"The thing about Nicole is that she is always taking the time to help others instead of herself," explains twenty-year-old Katie. She is one of Nicole's best friends and was among the first people to learn about her emotional problems. "Even when I ask about her depression, she turns the conversation back toward my life."

Katie suspects that balancing her concerns with Nicole's comfort is an example of the complicated situation that many people face. "We all want the person [we care about] to get better," she concludes. "But it's hard to know the best way to help without pushing too much or showing too little interest in his or her health. . . . The best that I can do is to remind Nicole that I'm here for her to talk to and to let her know that I want her to be happy and healthy. I try to send her text messages to check in on her so that she knows that someone is always looking out for her."

behavior—and especially the threat of suicide—can be both frightening and frustrating for everyone involved. Parents, siblings, educators, and peers commonly experience shock and guilt. They may become angry with themselves because they didn't notice or address the problem sooner.

Even after someone coping with depression or anxiety begins treatment, it is often challenging to reestablish relationships that are shaped

It is often hard to repair relationships impacted by depression or stress.

by trust, honesty, and respect. People working to overcome these mental conditions are frequently self-conscious. Some worry about being misjudged and misunderstood. They fear that they are taking more than they are giving by asking for ongoing patience and support.

Meanwhile, it is difficult for friends and family members not to be concerned. In fact, parents and peers tend to be more sensitive to symptoms of depression and anxiety after someone they know starts treatment for these issues. They worry about missing signs of problems that were perhaps overlooked in the past—and that the people they care about are struggling to avoid in the future.

FIVE

TACKLING TOUGH MENTAL CONDITIONS

SEVENTEEN-YEAR-OLD ANTHONY SAYS he still struggles with the pain of losing his best friend to suicide in 2009. After receiving treatment for his depression and stress, however, the Tennessee teen believes he's in a much better emotional position to cope with whatever challenges lay ahead of him.

"I will never get over the sudden death of my friend," he acknowledges. "I do get

> "I do get sad . . . at times, and life is going to throw unexpected things at me. . . . But I also think I have successfully fought the depression."
> — Anthony

sad and miss him at times, and life is going to throw unexpected things at me that could make me somewhat depressed. But I also think I have successfully fought the depression."

Anthony says that therapy played a large role in helping him get to this point. He admits that he was initially resistant to the idea of seeing a therapist. Yet he also grasped that his depression and the stress of bottling up his feelings were not simply going to disappear on their own. Eventually, Anthony's mom and dad made arrangements for him to begin working with a therapist to help him process his emotions.

"At first, I wasn't happy about any of this at all," he says. "It seemed stupid to just talk about what was wrong. But once I got my feelings out in the open, I felt so much better . . . like a huge weight was off my shoulders." Anthony adds that his therapist offered him practical ways to help reduce stress and depression on a day-to-day basis.

"She suggested [activities] that I could do to . . . take my

> "Once I got my feelings out in the open, I felt so much better . . . like a huge weight was off my shoulders."
> — Anthony

Some people turn to hobbies as a way to relieve stress or sadness.

mind off things," he recalls. "For example, I'm a big basketball guy, so she mentioned that I should go shoot some hoops to relieve stress."

Anthony emphasizes that both his present outlook and plans for the future are far brighter than they were before he sought treatment for his stress

47

STARTLING STAT

MENTAL-HEALTH EXPERTS BELIEVE THAT LESS THAN 33 PERCENT OF TEENS SUFFERING FROM DEPRESSION RECEIVE TREATMENT.

"My life since I've [done] therapy has been so much better than when I just kept everything inside."
— Anthony

and depression. "Life has really just been going great," he says. "My life since I've done therapy has been so much better than when I just kept everything inside."

AN OVERVIEW OF TREATMENT OPTIONS

Since not all sufferers share identical symptoms of clinical depression and stress, there is no single "cure" that magically helps everyone overcome these conditions. Treatment for serious depression and anxiety typically includes one or more types of therapy.

In many cases, a psychiatrist, psychologist, or counselor recommends that a person begins **psychotherapy**,

Therapy can be an extremely helpful tool in dealing with stress and depression.

or "talk therapy," to deal with severe depression or anxiety. During psychotherapy, therapists educate patients about their condition. They also encourage people suffering from clinical depression or anxiety to discuss their emotions and to explore more positive methods of coping with them.

The setting in which a patient receives treatment depends on a few factors. People who actively discuss or attempt suicide—or show any form of self-destructive

49

behavior that threatens their safety or the safety
of others—may do best in an inpatient treatment
program. It is often most practical for such individuals to at least begin therapy at a hospital or
recovery center, where therapists can closely moni-
tor their progress.

On the other hand, many patients dealing with
clinical depression or stress are able to participate in
less-intensive outpatient treatment. They work with
their therapists to schedule a set number of sessions
over a certain time period or until a particular goal
is accomplished. A patient involved in this type of
treatment may attend therapy in a wide range of
settings that include a doctor's office, a hospital, a
school, or a recovery and rehabilitation center. The
exact location of therapy is not as important as the
person's ability to comfortably communicate with
his or her therapist.

"Studies have shown that one of the biggest factors for creating change is the relationship between
the [patient] and the therapist," says Doctor Sachs. "I
would advise anyone seeking treatment to make sure
they feel at ease with their therapist. They should feel
like they can tell this person . . . anything."

"I would advise anyone seeking treatment to make sure they feel at ease with their therapist. They should feel like they can tell this person . . . anything."

— **George Sachs, PsyD**

MIXED OPINIONS ON MEDICATION

In addition to discussing their problems with professionals, some patients take certain medications as part of their treatment plan. Mental-health experts have divided opinions on the use of drugs to reduce the symptoms of depression and anxiety. Many feel that antidepressant and antianxiety medications can be helpful but should never be viewed as a substitute for therapy. Others worry that not enough is known about the possible side effects of these drugs—especially on a teen's developing body. People who prefer not to prescribe antidepressant and antianxiety medicines also point out that those drugs aren't always effective.

Reflections and Realizations

As someone who's dealt with anxiety from about age twelve, Matt—who is now thirty-two—firmly believes that a good therapist can change a person's life. Now a film archivist living in California, he feels he's come a long way since he initially began battling severe stress and depression. Matt says that he can trace the source of his problems to "general adolescence issues compounded by being gay and growing up in a very religious household." Though he admits that he "had always thought the very idea of therapy was depressing and strange" and not for him, he eventually began to change his mind.

"Now, even though I have my bad days, I am able to get through them," Matt says. He also has learned to use outside activities, such as volunteer work, as a way of relieving ongoing stress and depression. Looking back on his experiences with these conditions, he has a few words of advice for teenagers who may be suffering from them.

"You are not alone," he emphasizes. "Whatever you are going through, there are caring adults waiting to listen to you. High school is a rough time for any number of reasons, but you won't be there forever."

STARTLING STAT

ABOUT 47 PERCENT OF DEPRESSED ADOLESCENTS WHO
PARTICIPATED IN A RECENT MEDICAL STUDY ADMITTED TO
RELAPSING AFTER THEIR TREATMENT ENDED.

Yet not everyone is completely against using these medications to treat depression and anxiety. In fact, several doctors believe that prescription drugs frequently help patients have more meaningful experiences in therapy. By reducing the unpleasant symptoms that accompany severe depression and stress, they sometimes allow people to better focus on what is actually causing their problems.

Regardless of what makes up a patient's specific treatment plan, working to overcome clinical depression or anxiety can be a challenging and slow process. Some people take longer than others to change negative behaviors and attitudes that may be impacting their mental condition. In addition, balancing a treatment schedule with school and social activities is not always easy.

Nor does therapy or medication guarantee that sufferers will never have a recurrence of serious depression or stress. It is therefore important for patients to stay in contact with their doctor or therapist even if they no longer see them on a regular basis. Being aware of the symptoms of clinical depression and anxiety, as well as what triggers them, also helps people recognize and address a possible **relapse**.

SIX

TEENS' SOLUTIONS AND STRATEGIES

T HERE'S NO ONE SIMPLE SOLUTION that will suddenly wipe out serious depression and stress—or the triggers that cause them—among American teenagers. From the perspective of seventeen-year-old Paige, however, a good start would be changing the way people communicate with one another.

"I've heard so many times, 'You're not alone,'" says the Illinois teen. "But that's something you have to experience—not just hear. Once people start talking to each other [about their emotions], they often discover that we're all more similar than we think." Doctor Sachs backs up Paige's argument with his

56

own thoughts about why teenagers need to be encouraged to communicate more about what they are feeling.

"One fundamental way that people become depressed is by not verbalizing what they want and need," he explains. "Providing teens with more outlets for self-expression can be an important part of the solution. This may include increased counseling opportunities in schools and an encouragement of more dialogue [with family members] at home." Blogging, journaling, and joining school and community support groups are a few other options.

> "I've heard so many times, 'You're not alone,' but that's something you have to experience—not just hear."
> — Paige

STARTLING STAT

A 2010 STUDY REVEALED THAT ONLY 50 PERCENT OF YOUNG PEOPLE HAD TALKED TO THEIR PARENTS ABOUT STRESS OR WORRY THEY HAD EXPERIENCED OVER THE PREVIOUS MONTH.

Keeping a journal is one way to express feelings.

INCREASING SOCIAL AWARENESS

Eighteen-year-old Nicole agrees with Paige's and Sachs's observations. She also believes that it's important to continue educating society about depression and stress. Nicole feels that one of the most important ways of doing so is by increasing awareness about mental-health issues.

58

"Pamphlets addressing these topics should be [readily] available in hospitals, schools, and businesses," she emphasizes. "The media also needs to play a role. . . . When stars and celebrities open up about their depression and stress, the media should portray them positively and help show the public that there is nothing to be ashamed of. I think this would make more people willing to seek treatment."

Minds in Motion is a national campaign devoted to raising awareness about depression.

> "People get really, really good at masking their problems. What schools need to do is catch kids before they feel they need to cope with a mask." — **Nicole**

She adds that educating people about the realities of depression and anxiety would also benefit young sufferers.

"It would be truly helpful if teachers became more aware of what signs [of clinical depression and anxiety] to look for," she says. "People get really, really good at masking their problems. What schools need to do is catch kids before they feel they need to cope with a mask."

TEENS WHO TAKE ACTION

Like Nicole, seventeen-year-old Anthony is in favor of reaching out to teenagers before depression or

STARTLING STAT

MENTAL-HEALTH EXPERTS BELIEVE THAT DEPRESSION AND ANXIETY AFFECT UP TO 15 PERCENT OF PRESCHOOLERS.

stress results in serious problems. From his point of view, one way of accomplishing this goal is for people his age to become more proactive. For example, the Tennessee teen got together with his friends and recently created the Kenneth Andrew Thompson (K.A.T.) Foundation to address adolescent depression. The organization is named after Anthony's best friend, who committed suicide.

"We hope to have group sessions two or three times a month for anyone to . . . talk about whatever is bugging them," he explains. "We want to let teens know that there are people out there that love them very much. . . . We also want them to understand that it's okay to be depressed or sad and that we are here to help them or to get help for them." Anthony adds that members of the K.A.T. Foundation give presentations to school groups, as well.

> "We . . . want [teens] to understand that it's okay to be depressed or sad and that we are here to help them or to get help for them." — Anthony

"We are trying to get the word out there and talk about this subject that no one wants to talk about,"

It is important for people dealing with stress and depression to realize that they are not alone.

Show Your Support!

Since 1949, Americans have recognized May as Mental-Health Month. You can do your part to help raise awareness about depression and anxiety. Talk to school officials or community organizers about hanging posters or distributing fliers that list warning signs, statistics, and treatment options. Alternatively, think about starting your own local support group for teens who are dealing with depression or anxiety.

he says. "I hope to share my story and to . . . raise awareness. We also are currently working on organizing fundraisers and creating a website."

Anthony's story—along with those of Nicole and Paige—are proof that teenagers can and do overcome depression and stress. Their future lives may not always be easy. Yet they are certain to be filled with meaning and opportunities to encourage other young people struggling with similar issues.

Status Update on Teen Sources

As of mid-2011 . . .

ANTHONY indicated that he is doing well and plans to keep the K.A.T. Foundation going strong. He remains dedicated to making a difference in the lives of teens struggling with depression and stress.

NICOLE reported she is attending Loyola University in Chicago, Illinois, and plans to study sociology and anthropology. She says that her volunteer work to promote racial equality has been deeply therapeutic and brings added stability to her life.

PAIGE said that she is currently studying at Butler University in Indianapolis, Indiana. She stated that she continues to make a conscious effort to cope with her anxiety in a healty manner.

Notes

CHAPTER 1

p. 5, "was always a worrier": Nicole, personal interview, August 9, 2010.

p. 5, "happy mask": Nicole interview.

p. 6, "I like people thinking . . .": Nicole interview.

p. 6, "I rode my bike . . .": Nicole interview.

p. 8, "It suddenly occurred to me . . .": Nicole interview.

p. 9, "When I was at my worst . . .": Nicole interview.

p. 10, "A recent study revealed that . . .": statistical data on the percentage of teens who cite schoolwork as the source of their stress, quoted in Tim Parsons, "Guidebook Helps Adults in Baltimore Identify, Cope with Teen Stress," *JHU Gazette*, November 8, 2004, www.jhu.edu/~gazette/2004/08nov04/08teen.html.

p. 10, "is characterized by feelings of . . .": from the clinical definition of stress, "Teens in Distress Series: Adolescent Stress and Depression," University of Minnesota Extension, 2011 (specific date last updated not available), www.extension.umn.edu/distribution/youthdevelopment/da3083.html.

p. 10, "is characterized by more extreme . . .": from the clinical definition of depression, "Teens in Distress Series: Adolescent Stress and Depression."

p. 12, "Research shows that approximately . . .": statistical data on the percentage of teens dealing with clinical depression, "Adolescent Depression," National Alliance on Mental Illness (NAMI), December 2010,

www.nami.org/Content/ContentGroups/CAAC
/FamilyGuidePRINT.pdf.

p. 12, "Experts believe that . . .": statistical data on the
percentage of teens dealing with an anxiety disorder,
"Teen Stress Statistics," TeenHelp.com, 2011 (specific
date last updated not available), www.teenhelp.com
/teen-stress/stress-statistics.html.

p. 12, "Suicide is the third-leading . . .": statistical data on
how suicide ranks as a cause of death, "Depression
in Teens," National Mental Health Association
(NMHA), 2011 (specific date last updated not
available), www.nmha.org/index.cfm?objectid=
C7DF950F-1372-4D20-C8B5BD8DFDD94CF1.

p. 12, "Research indicates that as . . .": statistical data on
the percentage of teens who struggle with depression
for twelve-month periods, "Teenage Depression
Statistics," Teen Depression (specific date last updated
not available), www.teendepression.org/stats/teenage-
depression-statistics.

p. 13, "We all actually need . . .": Claudia Welke, personal
interview, January 22, 2011.

p. 14, "Are we seeing more depression . . .": Welke interview.

CHAPTER 2

p. 15, "really down all the time . . .": Anthony, personal
interview, January 13, 2011.

p. 15, "I didn't know what to . . .": Anthony interview.

p. 16, "Mental-health experts believe . . .": statistical data
on the increased likelihood that depressed teens will
commit suicide, "Teenage Depression Statistics."

p. 16, "To be honest, day-to-day . . .": Anthony interview.

p. 18, "having a problem": Anthony interview.

p. 18, "I think depression and stress . . .": Anthony interview.

p. 18, "Research indicates that between . . .": statistical
data on the percentage of depressed teens who have a
family history of mental-health problems, "Teenage
Depression Statistics."

p. 20, "There is not one single factor . . .": George Sachs,
personal interview, January 27, 2011.

p. 20, "Just because you have experienced . . .":
Sachs interview.

p. 24, "I don't know if I was ever . . .": Anthony interview,
January 26, 2011.

CHAPTER 3

p. 26, "periods of emotional instability": Paige, personal
interview, September 16, 2010.

p. 26, "running on empty battery": Paige interview.

p. 27, "Researchers say that about 19 . . .": statistical data
on the percentage of stressed teen girls who refuse
to address the source of their anxiety, "Teen Stress
Statistics."

p. 27, "hyperventilate in complete anxiety . . .": Paige
interview, January 23, 2011.

p. 27, "defeated, depleted, and depressed . . .": Paige interview.

p. 27, "During my panic attacks . . .": Paige interview.

p. 29, "It is not unusual for . . .": Welke interview.

p. 31, "A recent study shows . . .": statistical data on the
percentage of Americans who complain about having
physical symptoms as a result of their stress, "Americans

Too Stressed Out, Poll Finds," ConsumerAffairs.com,
October 25, 2007,
www.consumeraffairs.com/news04/2007/10
/stressed.html.

p. 32, "High school has always been . . .": Paige interview.

p. 32, "It's easy to forget why . . .": Paige interview.

CHAPTER 4

p. 35, "It's hard to keep . . .": Nicole interview.

p. 37, "Recent research indicates that . . .": statistical data
on the percentage of depressed women who are too
embarrassed to seek help, "Depression Statistics in
Men vs. Women," quoted in Gail Saltz, "Am I Just
Sad—or Truly Depressed?" TODAY.com, March 10,
2004, www.today.msnbc.msn.com/id/4489902/ns/
today-today_health/t/am-i-just-sad-or-truly-depressed.

p. 37, "I admitted some of . . .": Nicole interview.

p. 37, "[Those issues] started to . . .": Nicole interview.

p. 40, "During one mental-health study . . .": statistical data
on the percentage of teens who felt an increase in stress
levels (versus the percentage of their parents who were
aware of this change), "APA Stress Survey: Children
Are More Stressed Than Parents Realize," American
Psychological Association (APA), November 23, 2009,
www.apapracticecentral.org/update/2009/11-23/
stress-survey.aspx.

p. 41, "Sometimes teens isolate themselves . . .":
Sachs interview.

p. 42, "The thing about Nicole is . . .": Katie, personal
interview, January 28, 2011.

p. 42, "Even when I ask about . . .": Katie interview.

p. 47, "We all want the . . .": Katie interview.

CHAPTER 5

p. 45, "I will never get over . . .": Anthony interview.

p. 46, "At first, I wasn't . . .": Anthony interview.

p. 46, "She suggested [activities] that . . .": Anthony interview.

p. 48, "Mental-health experts believe . . .": statistical data on the percentage of depressed teens who receive treatment, "Teenage Depression Statistics."

p. 48, "Life has really just . . .": Anthony interview.

p. 50, "Studies have shown that . . .": Sachs interview.

p. 52, "general adolescence issues compounded . . .": Matt, personal interview, January 30, 2011.

p. 52, "had always thought the . . .": Matt interview.

p. 52, "Now, even though I . . .": Matt interview.

p. 52, "You are not alone . . .": Matt interview.

p. 54, "About 47 percent of . . .": statistical data on the percentage of depressed adolescents who relapse after receiving treatment, "One in Two Depressed Teens Prone to Recurrence after Recovery," Johns Hopkins Children's Center, November 1, 2010, www.hopkinschildrens.org/one-in-two-depressed-teens-prone-to-recurrence-after-recovery.aspx.

CHAPTER 6

p. 56, "I've heard so many times . . .": Paige interview, January 23, 2011.

p. 57, "One fundamental way that . . .": Sachs interview.

p. 57, "A 2010 study revealed . . .": statistical data on the

percentage of young people who had talked to their
parents about stress they had experienced over the
past month of their lives, "Key Findings," APA, 2011
(specific date last updated not available), www.apa.org
/news/press/releases/stress/key-findings.aspx.

p. 59, "Pamphlets addressing these topics . . .": Nicole
interview.

p. 60, "It would be truly . . .": Nicole interview.

p. 60, "Mental health experts believe that . . .": statistical
data on the percentage of preschoolers who are affected
by depression and anxiety, "Depression and Anxiety
Affect up to 15 Percent of Preschoolers, Canadian
Study Finds," Science Daily, August 30, 2009, www.
sciencedaily.com/releases/2009/08/090828104134.htm.

p. 61, "We hope to have . . .": Anthony interview.

p. 61, "We are trying to . . .": Anthony interview.

Glossary

anxiety a condition marked by disproportionate worry, emotional uncertainty, and physical disquiet

clinical depression depression so severe that it requires medical attention

comorbid referring to diseases or medical conditions, often unrelated, that a patient experiences at the same time

depressed suffering from a mental condition marked by often extreme hopelessness and sadness

eating disorder a condition in which anxiety about body image or weight distorts a person's normal eating pattern

hyperventilate to breathe abnormally quickly and deeply

peers people within a group who are markedly similar in age, income, education, or social position

psychotherapy a form of psychological medical treatment that typically involves communication with a therapist

relapse the return of symptoms or a disease that
was thought to be cured

stigma a mark or label that causes or is associated
with shame or disgrace

stressed suffering from an exaggeratedly high
level of emotional frustration

trauma a deeply upsetting emotional or physical
mishap or a prolonged disordered emotional
state traceable to such an event

Further Information

BOOKS

Biegel, Gina M. *The Stress Reduction Workbook for Teens: Mindfulness Skills to Help You Deal with Stress*. Oakland, CA: Instant Help Books, 2009.

Eagen, Rachel. *Suicide*. New York: Crabtree, 2011.

Lucas, Eileen. *More Than the Blues? Understanding and Dealing with Depression*. Berkeley Heights, NJ: Enslow, 2010.

Marsico, Katie. *Eating Disorders*. New York: Cavendish Square Publishing, LLC, 2014.

DVD

National Geographic. *Stress—Portrait of a Killer*, 2008.

WEBSITES

Palo Alto Medical Foundation—Stress

www.pamf.org/teen/life/stress

A website geared toward teens that provides a variety of tips for dealing with stress.

TeensHealth—Depression

www.kidshealth.org/teen/your_mind/mental_health /depression.html

A site that offers a closer look at signs, symptoms, and treatment options related to depression.

Bibliography

BOOKS

Bradley, Michael. *When Things Get Crazy with Your Teen: The Why, the How, and What to Do Now.* New York: McGraw-Hill, 2009.

Dingwell, Heath. *Forty-Six Things You Can Do to Help Your Teen Manage Stress.* Nashville, TN: Turner, 2010.

Edelman, Sarah. *Change Your Thinking: Overcome Stress, Combat Anxiety and Depression, and Improve Your Life with CBT.* New York: Marlowe, 2007.

Griffith, Gail. *Will's Choice: A Suicidal Teen, a Desperate Mother, and a Chronicle of Recovery.* New York: HarperCollins, 2005.

Hart, Archibald D., and Catherine Hart Weber. *Is Your Teen Stressed or Depressed?: A Practical and Inspirational Guide for Parents of Hurting Teens.* Nashville, TN: Thomas Nelson, 2008.

Robbins, Paul R. *Understanding Depression.* Jefferson, NC: McFarland, 2009.

ONLINE ARTICLES

"Adolescent Depression," National Alliance on Mental Illness (NAMI), December 2010 (specific date last updated not available), www.nami.org/ Content/ContentGroups/CAAC/ FamilyGuidePRINT.pdf.

"Americans Too Stressed Out, Poll Finds," ConsumerAffairs.com, October 25, 2007,

www.consumeraffairs.com/news04/2007/10/
stressed.html.

"APA Stress Survey: Children Are More Stressed Than
Parents Realize," American Psychological Association
(APA), November 23, 2009, www.apapracticecentral
.org/update/2009/11-23/stress-survey.aspx.

"APA Survey Raises Concern about Parent Perceptions of
Children's Stress," APA, November 3, 2009, www.apa
.org/news/press/releases/2009/11/stress.aspx.

"Depression and Anxiety Affect up to 15 Percent of
Preschoolers, Canadian Study Finds," ScienceDaily,
August 30, 2009, www.sciencedaily.com
/releases/2009/08/090828104134.htm.

"Depression in Teens," National Mental Health
Association (NMHA), 2011, www.nmha.org/
index.cfm?objectid=C7DF950F-1372-4D20-
C8B5BD8DFDD94CF1.

"Key Findings," APA, 2011, www.apa.org/news/press
/releases/stress/key-findings.aspx.

"One in Two Depressed Teens Prone to Recurrence
after Recovery," Johns Hopkins Children's Center,
November 1, 2010, www.hopkinschildrens.org/one-
in-two-depressed-teens-prone-to-recurrence-after-
recovery.aspx.

Parsons, Tim. "Guidebook Helps Adults in Baltimore
Identify, Cope with Teen Stress," *JHU Gazette*,
November 8, 2004, www.jhu.edu/~gazette/2004/
08nov04/08teen.html.

Saltz, Gail. "Am I Just Sad—or Truly Depressed?" TODAY
.com, March 10, 2004, www.today.msnbc.msn.com

/id/4489902/ns/today-today_health/t/am-i-just-sad-
or-truly-depressed.

"Teenage Depression Statistics," Teen Depression, www
.teendepression.org/stats/teenage-depression-statistics.
Specific date last updated not available.

"Teens in Distress Series: "Adolescent Stress and
Depression," University of Minnesota Extension,
2011, www.extension.umn.edu/distribution/
youthdevelopment/da3083.html. Specific date last
updated not available.

Teen Stress Statistics," TeenHelp.com, 2011, www.teenhelp
.com/teen-stress/stress-statistics.html. Specific date last
updated not available.

PERSONAL INTERVIEWS

Anthony. January 13, 2011; January 26, 2011.
Katie. January 29, 2011.
Matt. January 30, 2011.
Nicole. August 9, 2010; January 25, 2011; January 30, 2011.
Paige. September 16, 2010; January 23, 2011.
George Sachs, PsyD. January 27, 2011.
Claudia Welke, MD. January 22, 2011.

Index

Page numbers in **boldface** are illustrations.

About the Author

KATIE MARSICO has authored more than eighty books for children and young adults. She lives in Elmhurst, Illinois, with her husband and children.